Words
For
Women

SUMMERSDALE

Summersdale Publishers Ltd
46 West Street
Chichester
West Sussex
PO19 1RP
UK

Printed and bound in Great Britain

ISBN 1 873475 60 8

Jacket by Java Jive Design, Chichester.

Contents

Words For Women

by men

Age cannot wither her, nor custom stale
Her infinite variety: other women cloy
The appetites they feed, but she makes hungry,
Where most she satisfies.

Shakespeare
Antony and Cleopatra

Shall I lose
The privilege of my sex, which is my will,
To yield a reason like a man?

Massinger
A Very Woman

To cheat a man is nothing;
but the woman must have fine parts,
indeed, who cheats a woman.

John Gay
The Beggar's Opera

A noble man is led far
by a woman's gentle words.

Goethe
Iphigenia auf Tauris

Women may be whole oceans deeper than we are, but they are also a whole paradise better. She may have got us out of Eden, but as a compensation she makes the earth very pleasant.

John Oliver Hobbes
Ambassador

Let man say whate'er they will
Woman, woman, rules them still.

Isaac Bickerstaffe
The Sultan

I have always said it: Nature meant
woman to be her masterpiece.

Lessing
Emilia Galotti

The sweetest noise on earth,
a woman's tongue;
A string which hath no discord.

Bryan W. Procter
Rafaelle and Fornarina

As for the women, though we scorn and flout 'em,
We may live with, but cannot live without 'em.

Frederic Reynolds
The Will

My love in her attire doth show her wit,
   It doth so well become her;
For every season she hath dressings fit,
   For winter, spring and summer.
   No beauty she doth miss
   When all her robes are on;
   But beauty's self she is
   When all her robes are gone.

Anonymous Madrigal

Do you not know I am a woman?
When I think, I must speak.

Shakespeare
As You Like It

He is a fool who thinks by force or skill
To turn the current of a woman's will.

Calderon
Adventures of Five Hours

She can flourish staff or pen,
And deal a wound that lingers;
She can talk the talk of men,
And touch with thrilling fingers.

George Meredith
Marian

One woman reads another's character
Without the tedious trouble of deciphering.

Ben Jonson
New Inn

Whether they give or refuse, it delights
women to have been asked.

Ovid

Ars Amatoria. Book I

But take all women, good and bad,
There is this much about them
To keep this world as it is
We cannot live without them.

"Percy the Poet"
Why the Women Rule the Men

A woman should always stand by a woman.

Euripides
Helen

She walks in Beauty, like the night
Of cloudless climes and starry skies;
And all that's best of dark and bright
Meet in her aspect and her eyes.

Lord Byron
She Walks In Beauty

A cat has nine lives,
and a woman has nine cats' lives.

Thomas Fuller
Gnomologia

Ten measures of speech descended on the world; women took nine and men one.

Babylonian Talmud
Kiddushin

Would men but follow
what the sex advise,
All things would prosper,
all the world grow wise.

Pope
January and May

The most precious possession that ever comes
to a man in this world is a woman's heart.

J.G. Holland
Lessons in Life: Perverseness

Women represent the triumph of matter
over mind, just as men represent the
triumph of mind over morals.

Oscar Wilde
Portrait Of Dorian Gray

The majority of husbands remind me of an
orang-utan trying to play the violin.

Honoré de Balzac

O fairest of creation! last and best
Of all God's works! creature in whom excell'd
Whatever can to sight or thought be form'd,
Holy, divine, good, amiable, or sweet!

John Milton
Paradise Lost

Woman, they say, was only made of man:
Methinks 'tis strange they should be so unlike!
It may be all the best was cut away,
To make the woman, and the naught was left
Behind with him.

Beaumont & Fletcher
Scornful Lady

Nature has given woman so much power that
the law has very wisely given them little.

Samuel Johnson
Letters Vol I

I have but one simile, and that's a blunder,
For wordless woman, which is silent thunder.

Lord Byron
Don Juan

Women, you know, do seldom fail
To make the stoutest men turn tail.

Samuel Butler
Hudibras

The silliest woman can manage a clever man; but it needs a very clever woman to manage a fool.

Rudyard Kipling
Plain Tales From the Hills

It is a woman's reason to say I will
do such a thing because I will.

Jeremiah Burroughes
On Hosea

If it was woman who took man out of Paradise,
it is still woman, and woman only, who can
lead him back.

Elbert Hubbard
Epigrams

No friendship is so cordial or delicious as
that of girl for girl; no hatred so intense and
immovable as that of woman for woman.

W. S. Landor
Imaginary Conversations: Epicurus, Leontion and Ternisa

Women and elephants never forget an injury.

H. H. Munro (Saki)
Reginald on Besetting Sins

Man was made when Nature
was but an apprentice, but woman
when she was a skilful mistress of her art.

Edward Sharpham
Cupid's Whirligig

My lady's presence makes the roses red
Because to see her lips they blush for shame;
The lily's leaves, for envy, pale became,
For her white hands in them this envy bred.

Henry Constable
Sonnet

Was this the face that launched a thousand ships
And burnt the topless towers of Ilium?
Sweet Helen, make me immortal with a kiss.

Christopher Marlowe
Doctor Faustus

No one knows like a woman how to say things that
are at once gentle and deep.

Victor Hugo

O! let me have thee whole — all — all — be mine!
That shape, that fairness, that sweet minor zest
Of love, your kiss — those hands, those eyes divine,
That warm, white, lucent, million-pleasured breast.

John Keats
To Fanny

So beautiful – God himself quailed
at her approach: the long body curved
like the horizon.

R. S. Thomas
The Woman

England is the paradise of women, the purgatory
of men, and the hell of horses.

John Florio

Her two shy knees bound in a single trouser,
With, 'twixt her lips, a violet
Perched as a proxy for a cigarette,
She takes her window in our smoking carriage,
And scans us, calmly scorning men and marriage.

Coventry Patmore
The Girl of all Periods: An Idyll

Heav'n has no rage, like love to hatred turned,
Nor Hell a fury, like a woman scorned.

William Congreve
The Mourning Bride

What would men be without women?
Scarce, sir, mighty scarce.

Mark Twain

Duchess of Berwick: Our husbands would really forget our existence if we didn't nag at them from time to time, just to remind them that we have a perfect legal right to do so.

Oscar Wilde
Lady Windemere's Fan

Women have more imagination than men.
They need it to tell us how wonderful we are.

Arnold H. Glasow

Every man who is high up loves to think
he has done it all himself; and the wife smiles,
and lets it go at that. It's our only joke.
Every woman knows that.

J. M. Barrie
What Every Woman Knows

Brigands demand your money or your life;
women require both.

Samuel Butler

She is Venus when she smiles;
But she's Juno when she walks;
And Minerva when she talks.

Ben Jonson

The most important thing women have to do is
stir up the zeal of women themselves.

John Stewart Mill

On the seashore, with storm impending,
how envious was I of the waves
each in tumultuous turn descending
to lie down at her feet like slaves!

A. Pushkin
Eugene Onegin

. . . men act and women appear. Men look at
women. Women watch themselves
being looked at.

John Berger
Ways of Seeing

Who loves not women, wine and song
Remains a fool his whole life long.

Attributed to Martin Luther

Being a woman is a terribly difficult trade, since it
consists principally of dealing with men.

Joseph Conrad

Let no man value at a little price
A virtuous woman's counsel; her wing'd spirit
Is feather'd oftentimes with heavenly words.

Chapman
The Gentleman Usher

O woman! Lovely woman! Nature made thee
To temper man: we had been brutes without you.

Thomas Otway
Venice Preserved

If the heart of a man is depressed with cares,
The mist is dispell'd when a woman appears.

John Gay
The Beggar's Opera

Loveliest of women! Heav'n is in thy soul,
Beauty and virtue shine for ever round thee,
Brightening each other: thou art all divine.

Addison
Cato

A woman dares all things
when she loves or hates.

St. Jerome
Epistles: Valerius to Rufinus

There is something in a woman beyond all human delight; a magnetic virtue, a charming quality, an occult and powerful motive.

Robert Burton
Anatomy of Melancholy

I am a woman! nay, a woman wrong'd!
And when our sex from injuries take fire,
Our softness turns to fury – and our thoughts
Breathe vengeance and destruction.

Richard Savage
Sir Thomas Overbury

Without women the world would be like a
palette set in the raw umber and white.
Women are the colouring matter,
the glaze the old painters used.

George Moore
Ave

For the female of the species is
more deadly than the male.

Rudyard Kipling

Mrs Cheveley: [...] women are never disarmed by compliments. Men always are. That is the difference between the two sexes.

Lord Goring: Women are never disarmed by anything, as far as I know them.

Oscar Wilde
An Ideal Husband

There is a strong and ineradicable male
instinct that a learned, or even an
accomplished young woman is the most
intolerable monster in creation.

Male reviewer
The Saturday Review, 1864

O the opal and the sapphire of that wandering
western sea,
And the woman riding high above with bright hair
flapping free –
The woman whom I loved so, and who loyally
loved me.

Thomas Hardy
Beeny Cliff

So with a downcast mien and laughing voice
I followed, followed the swing of her white dress
That rocked in a lilt along; I watched the poise
Of her feet as they flew for a space,
then paused to press
The grass deep down with the royal burden of her;
And gladly I'd offered my breast to the tread of her.

D. H. Lawrence
Snap-Dragon

Be good, sweet maid, and let who can be clever;
Do lovely things, not dream them, all day long;
And so make Life, and Death, and that For Ever
One grand sweet song.

Charles Kingsley
A Farewell

Who is't can read a woman?

William Shakespeare
Cymbeline

The Woman Soul leadeth us Upward and on.

Goethe
Faust

That the woman was made of a rib out of the side of Adam; not out of his feet to be trampled upon by him, but out of his side to be equal with him, under his arm to be protected, and near his heart to be loved.

Matthew Henry
Note on Genesis

Earth's noblest thing, a Woman perfected.

J. R. Lowell
Irene

She is her self of best things the collection.

Sir Philip Sidney
Arcadia

The virtue of her lively looks
    Excels the precious stone;
I wish to have none other books
    To read or look upon.

Unknown
Songs and Sonnets

Now in hot, now in cold,
Full woeful is the household
That wants a woman.

Unknown
Towneley Plays

Words
For
Women

by women

What is woman? Only one of
Nature's agreeable blunders.

Hannah Cowley
Who's the Dupe?

If thou must love me, let it be for nought
Except for love's sake only. Do not say
"I love her for her smile . . . her look . . . her way
Of speaking gently . . . for a trick of thought
That falls in well with mine, and certes brought
A sense of pleasant ease on such a day"

Elizabeth Barrett Browning
Sonnet

A woman is like a tea-bag. You can't tell how strong she is until you put her in hot water.

Nancy Reagan

The people I'm furious with are the women's liberationists. They keep getting up on soapboxes and proclaiming women are brighter than men. That's true, but it should be kept quiet or it ruins the whole racket.

Anita Loos

I would venture to guess that Anon,
who wrote so many poems without
signing them, was often a woman.

Virginia Woolf
A Room of One's Own

Women have their faults
Men have only two;
Everything they say
And everything they do.

Anon

The first time Adam had a chance,
he laid the blame on Eve.

Nancy Astor

Man forgives woman anything save
the wit to outwit him.

Minna Antrim

Let us love dogs; let us love only dogs!
Men and cats are such unworthy creatures.

Marie Konstantinovna

They talk about a woman's sphere,
As though it had a limit.
There's not a place in heaven
There's not a task to mankind given
Without a woman in it.

Kate Field

A priest can achieve great victories with an army
of women at his command.

Mary Elizabeth Braddon

They tell me nothing but lies here, and they
think they can break my spirit. But I believe
what I choose and say nothing. I am not
so simple as I seem.

Catherine of Aragon
Letter to King Ferdinand of Spain

Though he had Eden to live in,
Man cannot be happy alone.

Josephine Pollard

O, love, in your sweet name enough
Illusory pretentious stuff
is talked and written.

Anne Finch
Essays on Marriage

It's the good girls who keep diaries –
the bad girls never have the time.

Tallulah Bankhead

It is a truth universally acknowledged
that a single man in possession of a good
fortune, must be in want of a wife.

Jane Austen
Pride and Prejudice

The male is a domestic animal,
which if trained with firmness and kindness,
can be trained to do most things.

Jilly Cooper

To love you without stint and all I can
Today, tomorrow, world without an end:
To love you much, and yet to love you more,
As Jordan at its flood sweeps either shore;
Since woman is the helpmeet made for man.

Christina Rossetti
Sonnet

All too many men still believe that
what feels good to them is automatically
what feels good to a woman.

Shere Hite

If civilisation is to advance at all in the future it must be through the help of women . . . women with the full power to work their way in society.

Emily Pankhurst

Women have served all these centuries as
looking-glasses possessing the magic and
delicious power of reflecting the figure of a man
at twice its natural size.

Virginia Woolf
A Room of One's Own

I am extraordinarily patient,
providing I get my own way in the end.

Margaret Thatcher

Women are never stronger than when they
arm themselves with their weaknesses.

Madame Du Defand
Letter to Voltaire

Nay, let the silence of my womanhood
Commend my woman-love to thy belief,
Seeing that I stand unwon, however wooed,
And render the garment of my life, in brief,
By a most dauntless, voiceless fortitude,
Lest one touch of this heart convey its grief.

Elizabeth Barrett Browning
Sonnet

The next Christ will perhaps be a female Christ.

Florence Nightingale
Cassandra

Then let us have our liberty again,
And challenge to yourselves no Sovreignty;
You came not in the world without our pain,
Make that a bar against your cruelty;
Your fault being greater, why should you disdain
Our being your equals, free from tyranny?

Emilia Lanier
Eve's Apology

Woman is all that man is not:
woman is not all that man is.

Joyce Carol Oates
Mysteries of Winterhurn

Why should marriage bring only tears?
All I wanted was a man
With a single heart,
And we would stay together
As our hair turned white.
Not somebody always after wriggling fish
With his big bamboo rod.

Chuo Wen-Chun
A Song Of White Hair

She would have despised the modern idea of
women being equal to men. Equal, indeed!
She knew they were superior.

Elizabeth Gaskell
Cranford

I am convinced that there is no difference between men and women, as there is no difference in their respiratory systems.

Nathalie Sarraute

. . . women have been called Queens for a
long time, but the kingdom given them
isn't worth ruling.

Louisa May Alcott

If things were even worse than they are after all this war they might have laid the blame upon the rule of a woman; but if such persons are honest they should blame only the rule of men who desire to play the part of kings. In future, if I am not any more hampered, I hope to show that women have a more sincere determination to preserve the country than those who have plunged it into the miserable condition to which it has been brought.

Catherine de Medici
Letter to Ambassador of Spain

A mother's love! O holy boundless thing!
Fountain whose waters never cease to spring.

Marguerite Blessington

Love is the whole history in a woman's life,
it is not an episode in a man's.

Germaine de Staël

For women there are, undoubtedly,
great difficulties in the path, but so much
the more to overcome. First no woman
should say, 'I am but a woman!' But a woman!
What more can you ask to be.

Maria Mitchell

She turned her face seaward to gather in an impression of space and solitude, which the vast expanse of water, meeting and melting with the moonlit sky, conveyed to her excited fancy. As she swam she seemed to be reaching out for the unlimited in which to lose herself.

Kate Chopin
Awakenings

Whatever women do, they must do twice
as well as men to be thought half as good.
Luckily, this is not difficult.

Charlotte Whitton

Woman has the same erect countenance as man,
the same ideals, the same love of beauty, honor,
the same wish for self-development, the same
longing after righteousness, and yet she is to be
imprisoned in an empty soul of which the very
windows are shut.

Anna van Schurman

I find nothing more extravagant than to see a
husband who is still in love with his wife.

Madeleine de Scudéry
An Excellent Romance

. . . man was created of the dust of the earth,
but woman was made of part of man, after that he
was living soule; yet was shee not produced from
Adam's foote, to be his too low inferior; nor from
his head to be his superiour, but from his side,
neare his heart, to be his equal.

Rachel Speght
Essay

We are the grief of man, in that we take all the grief from men: we languish when they laugh, we lie sighing when they sit singing, and sit sobbing when they lie slugging and sleeping.

Jane Anger
Protection for Women

Fervour is not placed in feelings but in will
to do well, which women may have as well as men.
There is no such difference between men
and women that women may not do great
things as we have seen by example of many
saints who have done great things.

Mary Ward

Marriage is a lottery in which men stake their
liberty and women their happiness.

Renée de Chateauneuf Rieux

God is a light to our feet. Let us not be
troubled by men, for what is man if not a
fleeting shadow, a windblown leaf, a fading flower,
and vanishing smoke!

Olimpia Morata
Last letter to Lavinia della Rovere

. . . suppress this violence of emotion. I have always found it best to appear to yield. Assume a seeming conformity to your husband's will, even attend mass, and you will more easily get the reins into your own hands.

Catherine de Medici
Remark to Queen of Navarre

Had I a beard I would have been the King of France. I have been defrauded by that confounded Salic law.

Renée de France

You remind me that the Apostle Paul told women
to be silent in Church. I would remind you of the
word of this same apostle that in Christ there is
no longer male nor female.

Katherine Zell
Entschuldigung Katherina Schutzinn

If it were customary to send little
girls to school and to teach them
the same subjects as are taught to boys,
they would learn just as fully and would
understand the subtleties of all arts
and sciences. Indeed, maybe they would
understand them better . . . for just as
women's bodies are softer than men's,
so their understanding is sharper.

Christine de Pisan
La Cité des Dames

. . . the lady ought to do exactly for her lover
as he does for her, without regard to rank;
for between two friends neither one should rule.

Marie de Ventadorn

It will not be the first time, Britons, that you have
been victorious under the conduct of your
Queen. For my part, I come not here as one
descended of royal blood, not to fight for
empire or riches, but as one of the common
people, to avenge the loss of their liberty, the
wrongs of myself and children.

Boadicea

I'll not listen to reason . . . reason always means
what someone else has got to say.

Elizabeth Gaskell

Fool! Don't you see that I could have
poisoned you a hundred times had I
been able to live without you!

Cleopatra

But nature be thanked, she has been so bountiful
to us as we oftener enslave men than men
enslave us. They seem to govern the world, but
we really govern the world in that we govern men.
For what man is he that is not governed by a
woman, more or less?

Margaret Cavendish

Ah, sentiments of mercy are in unison with a
woman's heart.

Catherine de Medici

Granted that the woman of the middle class
has now some leisure, some education, and
some liberty to investigate the world in which
she lives, it will not be in this generation or
in the next that she will have adjusted her
position or given a clear account of her
powers. 'I have the feelings of a woman,'
says Bathsheba in *Far from the Madding Crowd*,
'but I have only the language of men.'

Virginia Woolf
Men and Women

Obtain power, then, by all means;
power is the law of man; make it yours.

Maria Edgeworth

One is happy as a result of one's own efforts,
once one knows the necessary ingredients of
happiness — simple tastes, a certain degree of
courage, self denial to a point, love of work, and,
above all, a clear conscience. Happiness is no
vague dream, of that I now feel certain.

George Sand
Correspondance

If men cannot cope with women in the
medical profession let them take an
humble occupation in which they can.

Sara Josepha Hale

And from the soul three faculties arise,
The mind, the will, the power;
then wherefore shall
A woman have her intellect in vain,
Or not endeavor knowledge to attain.

Rachel Speght

If you do not tell the truth about yourself,
you cannot tell it about other people.

Virginia Woolf
The Moment and Other Essays

If the first woman God ever made
was strong enough to turn the world upside
down, all alone,
together women ought to be able to turn it
rightside up again.

Sojourner Truth
Ain't I a Woman?

No coward soul is mine,
No trembler in the world's storm-troubled
sphere:
I see Heaven's glories shine,
And faith shines equal, arming me from fear.

Emily Brontë
Last Lines

The perfection of outward loveliness is the soul
shining through its crystalline covering.

Jane Porter

In mother, wife, sister, sweetheart, lies the most precious part of men. In them he sees perpetual reminders of the death-sin, guarantees of immortality. Think, woman, what your existence means to man; dwell well on your responsibility.

Ray Frank

Love largely and hate nothing. Hold no aim
That does not chord with universal good.

Ella Wheeler Wilcox

She has need of a strong reason, of a truly Christian and well-tempered spirit, of all the assistance the best education can give her, and ought to have some good assurance of her own firmness and virtue, who ventures on such a trial; and for this reason 'tis less to be wondered at that women marry off in haste, for perhaps if they took time to consider and reflect upon it, they seldom would marry.

Mary Astell
Some Reflections upon Marriage

A woman here leads fainting Israel on,
She fights, she wins, she triumphs with a song,
Devout, majestic, for the subject fit,
And far above her arms, exalts her wit,
Then to the peaceful, shady palm withdraws,
And rules the rescued nation with her laws.

Anne Finch, Countess of Winchelsea
The Introduction

Gentle ladies, you will remember till old age what
we did together in our brilliant youth!

Sappho

I am more afraid of making a fault in my Latin, than of the Kings of Spain, France, Scotland, the whole House of Guise, and all of their confederates.

Elizabeth I

In losing a husband, one loses a master
who is often an obstacle to the
enjoyment of many things.

Madeleine de Scudéry

Let such as say our Sex is Void of Reason,
Know 'tis a Slander now, but once was Treason.

Anne Bradstreet

The entire social order [. . .] is arrayed against a woman who wants to rise to a man's reputation.

Germaine de Staël

I consider every attempt to induce women
to think they have a just right to participate
in the public duties of government as injurious
to their best interests and derogatory to
their character. Our empire is purer,
more excellent and spiritual.

Sara Josepha Hale

Father asked us what was God's noblest work.
Anna said men, but I said babies.
Men are often bad; babies never are.

Louisa May Alcott